Rescue Vehicles

Mary Kate Doman

Enslow Elementary
an imprint of

Enslow Publishers, Inc.
40 Industrial Road
Box 398
Berkeley Heights, NJ 07922
USA

http://www.enslow.com

For Liam, who loves things that go

Enslow Elementary, an imprint of Enslow Publishers, Inc.

Enslow Elementary® is a registered trademark of Enslow Publishers, Inc.

Library of Congress Cataloging-in-Publication Data

Doman, Mary Kate, 1979–
  Rescue vehicles / by Mary Kate Doman.
      p. cm. — (All about big machines)
  Includes index.
  Summary: "Learn how rescue vehicles are used"—Provided by publisher.
  ISBN 978-0-7660-3934-6
  1. Emergency vehicles—Juvenile literature. 2. Rescue work—Juvenile literature. I. Title.
  TL235.8.D65 2012
  629.222'34—dc23
                              2011014639

Paperback ISBN 1-978-1-59845-244-0

Printed in the United States of America

Phtoto credits: © 2011 Photos.com, a division of Getty Images. All rights reserved, pp 12–13, 22–23; Ivan Cholakov Gostock-dot-net/Shutterstock.com , pp. 10–11; Jeff Thrower/Shutterstock.com, pp.4–5; Shutterstock.com, title page, 6–7, 9, 14–15, 16–17, 18–19, 20–21

Cover Photo Credit: Mike Brake/Shutterstock.com

Note to Parents and Teachers

Help pre-readers get a jumpstart on reading. These lively stories introduce simple concepts with repetition of words and short simple sentences. Photos and illustrations fill the pages with color and effectively enhance the text. Free Educator Guides are available for this series at www.enslow.com. Search for the *All About Big Machines* series name.

Contents

Words to Know

ambulance   **siren**   **vehicles**

921

AMBULAN

NSWI
VOL
UE SQU

Rescue vehicles help people.

Rescue vehicles have bright lights.

They help people see them.

Rescue vehicles have loud sirens too.

They help people hear them.

Rescue vehicles save people.

Fire trucks help put out fires.

13

Police cars help
keep the city safe.

Ambulances help when people get hurt.

Lifeboats rescue people lost at sea.

Rescue vehicles help people everyday.

Rescue vehicles save people everyday.

Read More

Bingham, Caroline. *Big Book of Rescue Vehicles.* New York: Dorling Kindersley Publishing, 2000.

Coppendale, Jean. *Fire Trucks and Rescue Vehicles.* Ontario, Canada: Firefly Books Ltd., 2010.

Lindeen, Carol K. *Fire Trucks.* Mankato, MN: Capstone, 2005.

Web Sites

Enchanted Learning: Transportation Theme Page
<http://www.enchantedlearning.com/themes/transportation.shtml>

Sparky the Fire Dog's Fire Truck
<http://www.sparky.org/firetruck>

Index

Guided Reading Level: C
Guided Reading Leveling System is based on the guidelines recommended by Fountas and Pinnell.

Word Count: 64